Art by Denise Lawrence

Photograph by Joe Omelchuck

Sanctuary

A large percentage of spirits on earth.
Consumed by religion.
A soul and body hurt.
Was it the dark ages,
When the concept was formed,
That a church is ground for
Sanctuary?

Is that why many sprint to their doors?
Never is forgot
That family of trees.
The Redwood Clan is My
Sanctuary.

White Eagle

Starting at the Top

Be Here Then

A Brief History of Rhyme

Phillip Daly

AuthorHouse™
1663 Liberty Drive
Bloomington, IN 47403
www.authorhouse.com
Phone: 1-800-839-8640

2nd Edition

© 2010 Phillip Daly. All rights reserved.

No part of this book may be reproduced, stored in a retrieval system, or transmitted by any means without the written permission of the author.

First published by AuthorHouse 4/27/2010

ISBN: 978-1-4490-3648-5 (sc)

Printed in the United States of America
Bloomington, Indiana

This book is printed on acid-free paper.

papadaly1@gmail.com
713-249-1903

PHIL

**a.k.a.
WHITE EAGLE**

**a.k.a.
SIRI NATH SINGH KHALSA.**

Outline

I. MUSIC   *1*

Death's Ascension   *3*
I'm a List Person   *4*
Writing in Tongues   *5*
My Tattoo   *6*
A Fate Worse Than Life   *7*
Eyes Blink   *8*
Thoughts Not Known   *9*
Friends of Birds   *11*
Cheap Chirp   *12*
Morrisonesque   *13*

II. ROACHES   *15*

The Exterminator   *17*
Roach On The Ceiling   *18*

III. PETS   *21*

Who   *23*
I Love Fleas   *24*
Gizmo Spats 1 & 2   *25*
Dogs Don't Work   *26*
The Tingler / Renaissance   *27*
Nine Lives   *28*

IV. INDIANS   *29*

Border Line   *31*
Who What Where When Why If   *32*
The Eagle Has Landed   *33*

V. POLITICS   35

*Year Of The Busch or Is Addiction a Reflection Of
    Our Crazy Earth*   37
Pentagon vs. Pentangle   38
The Hole   39
(KW)(Kill A What?)   40
NAFTA or Night Asks For The Answer   41
B.S. In Politics   42
Now I'm Pissed   43
End of Politics/Sportscast   44

VI. SPORTS   47

Forward Pass   49
The Blitz   50
*Birth And Death In Houston With No Major Sports
    Win*   51
In Case I Die   52
Ticker Tape Day   53

VII. RELIGION   55

Philism   57
Religion   58
Redwood Sanctuary   59
Vatican Explosion   60
For Those Who Don't Know   61

VIII. DEVILS   63

Devils   65

IX. ANGELS   67

Flying   69

X. MY CHILD 71

The Earth Is Flat 73
Alone Not Together 74
A – Mongolians 75
Reason To Live 76
Everyday 77
To Shabd 78
10th Birthday Prayer 79
Over The Cliff 80
Drop 81
Mid Night X Mass 82
Relative-ity 83

XI. HER TO ME 87

My Father 89
My Daddy 90

XII. CHILDREN 93

A B C's 95
Adam Lost, A Damn Loss. America's Least Wanted. 96
Neighbors 97

XIII. SEX 99

Homework 101

XIV. CARDS 103

Gin 105

XV. FRIENDS 107

Annette O'Toole 109

Cruz	*110*
Recycle Man/St. Nick – A Christmas Gift	*111*
J. B. McCoy	*112*
12 10 93	*113*
Lost Comb = Lost Awareness	*114*
The Boat	*115*
For Hari & Me(Huddy)	*116*
Hands Shake	*117*
Bless Me Father	*118*
Jeff & Laticia	*119*
Who Was That Masked Man	*120*
Frogs	*121*
Lips	*122*

XVI. STEALING A WANTED POSTER OF PATTY HEARST FROM THE DOWNTOWN POST OFFICE – A MISDEMEANOR **125**

The Wind	*127*

XVII. CONFUSION / SAY **129**

No #	*131*
Puppets	*132*
Skeletons	*133*
Input	*134*
L A T E	*135*
Convenience Stores	*136*
La Strada(August 16, 1992)	*137*
Morning	*138*
Check Out	*139*
Tears	*140*
PA	*141*
Xcess	*142*
Laws	*143*

Bottoms Up	*144*
Finite vs. Infinite	*145*
L.A.	*146*
Remember When	*147*
Sounds of Music	*148*

XVIII. ME, MYSELF & I	***151***
Whatever, And That's Me	*153*
Socks	*154*
The Answer	*155*
Never Alone or We're All In This Together	*156*
Ground Zero / Starting At The Top	*157*
Karma	*158*
OM (Where The Heart Is)	*159*
A Prayer For Phil	*160*
Competition	*161*
Condominium	*162*
Angel's Puppet	*163*
Byzantine Empire	*165*
Red, White and Black	*167*
Mo Ho Tells	*168*
Winter Simmers	*169*
Dust	*170*
Secret	*171*
Three Meals A Day	*172*
P.S. Be Here Then For Baba Ram Dass	*173*
Master of Deceit or The Art of Lying	*174*
Poetry - - The Motion	*175*
Nats On Life	*176*
Time To Bite	*177*
Rat Race	*179*
Famousisity	*180*
Tomorrow	*181*
Greetings	*182*

Clan Of Kennedy	*183*
The Pain Of The Moment	*184*
News	*185*
POET/POEM	*186*
The Thinker	*187*
For Denise/Grasshopper	*188*
Mama Got The Belt	*189*
A Brief History of Rhyme	*190*
Child Abuse	*191*
LOVE	*192*
Homeless In Hyannisport	*193*
I Don't Fight With Food	*194*
Lordy, Lordy, Look Who's Forty	*195*

XIX. GOD AND JESUS   ***197***

Tools Of The Trade	*199*
Life	*200*
Empower All With All	*201*
Birth And Death Of Jesus	*202*
Rut	*203*
Jesus Or Hammer Time	*204*
Baba Ga Noose	*205*
Ism's	*206*
Home	*207*
Listerine	*208*
The Meaning Of Christmas	*209*
Here And There	*210*
For What I Don't Know	*211*
The Eyes Don't Have It	*212*
Upper Level Disturbance	*213*

XX. MY FIRST AND LAST WILL AND TESTAMENT **215**

My First And Last Will And Testament — *217*
Two Birds Look To The Sky Hi Come! — *218*
Intro To Blind Big Cake Carver/The End Is the Beginning — *219*

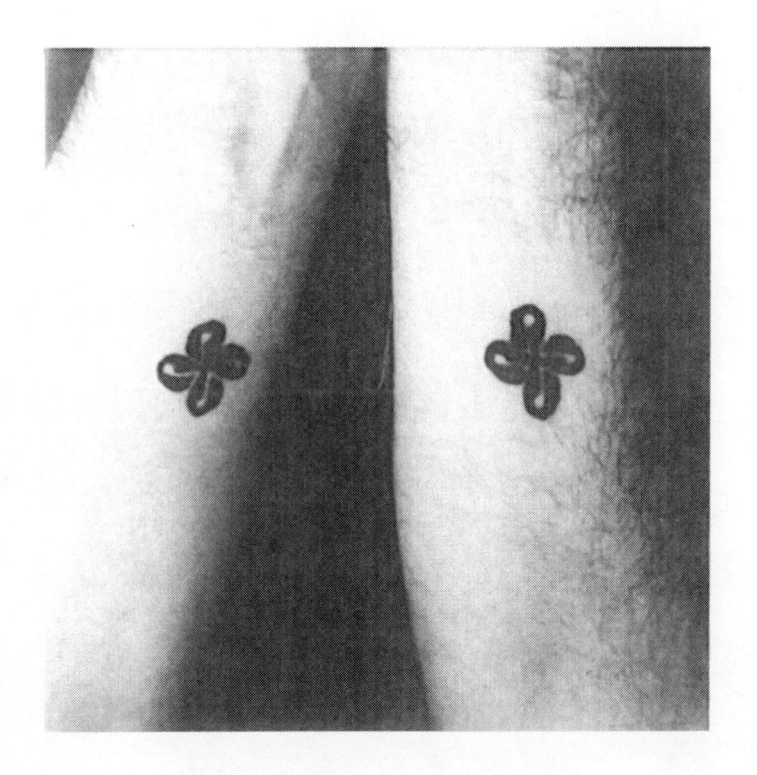

Photograph by Joe Omelchuck

I. MUSIC

Death's Ascension

If
God and the Devil
are really just the same,
let's get 'em in a band with us,
put Rock'N'Roll to shame.

We'll call it Death's Ascension,
find out what is next,
and when this body's gone,
we'll
PRAY THAT THERE IS REST.

I'm a List Person

When the list is over,
light up my fire, my funeral pyre;
well, the list it is my special friend,
it seems I write it down
and then I write it again
until the end.

It's like reading the paper;
the same old news
throughout history,
the same old abuse.

We come and we go,
the light we all know.

We feel it inside,
some of the time.

There is no end.

There is no end.

Writing in Tongues

See me deliver, a Thought I don't think.
It comes from a vacuum, don't wink.
Open your eyes and listen to others.
Your world can change;
it needn't be drothers.
What does it mean – the word above?
I won't look it up,
but faith is love.

You see I am crazy
to have faith in others.
Religion's majority – they are the others.
I was one of them,
actually twice.
There won't be a third time.
Never thrice.

Twice I was married,
never again.
Institutions are names.
Love never ends.

Each morning I rise
amidst the rubble.
In this city of siege,
there is always trouble.

Take one instant or maybe two
to ponder
this Gift,
GOD
will see me through.

My Tattoo

My Mark is my Soul.

Shame is gone.

I feel with my eyes.

Right needs wrong.

A musical monk,

Seems appropae.

I love Rock'N'Roll.

It's Spirit I crave.

(Notes of Sound)
Shrouded
In
Spirit

A Fate Worse Than Life

Why can't all <u>know</u>
Key Word
in
this
Show
Or
Play
the
Tune Unheard
FORALL.
Not just me,
I and Others
wait now,

PLEASE						LISTEN.

Eyes Blink

Eyes blink
involuntarily.

Breath.

Mother Theresa

is

Life Itself.

Feel

all

Pain.

SWEAT, BLOOD and TEARS.

Chords

chime

in three's.

Incorporation of the Hereafter.

Hi Ber Nate.

Thoughts Not Known

Beyond the concept

of a Thought,

is there

SOMETHING?

A

NOTE

for ALL,

of Course.

Photograph by Joe Omelchuck

Friends of Birds

Have you noticed that friends change?
They come and go, a few stay.
Family struggles.
In some lives, abuse and hurt.
Usually lies.

Give us Music
to soothe the pain.
Symphony, Rap, New Age,
Gospel, Rock, Jazz, Reggae.
Bluegrass, Zydeco, Opera,
Blues, Johnny Cash, Big Band,
Avant Garde, Punk, Heavy Metal,
see my hair fly.
Let's blend them together.

Music is life.
It is the real soul.

The Birds only sing.
Talk,
they don't know.
Can they lie and
ponder the pain?

I presume not to know.

Pray
fly
me
their
way.

Cheap Chirp

Whoever it may enlighten.
I'm First.

O.K. God.

I'm back again.

The monkey's on your back.

Humanity's in need.

I speak for myself.

That's what I've been told.

But the outlaw

of my mind

is becoming

bold.

So give me the Cliff Notes,

I'll sell them cheap.

No pulpit will have me.

Your knowledge I'll Free.

CHEAP.
CHIRP.

Morrisonesque

Rabbits, Indians,

Words, Music, Experience

Drawn
For
A
Chosen
Few.

Hotel Written,

Morrison

View.

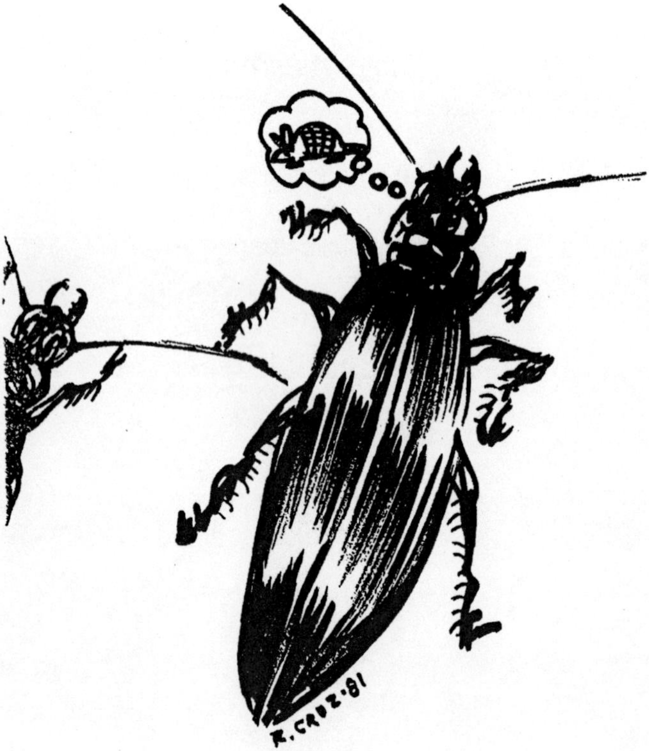
R. CRUZ·81

II. ROACHES

The Exterminator

One night a roach approached

I did not Kill.

Instead,

We Struck a Deal.

I said,

"I Won't Squash Your Face

If

You Keep Other Roaches Away."

It said,

"I'll Take Care of That,

But You Must Plug All Holes But One."

I said,

"Does That Mean I Must Caulk All Cracks

Save One?"

It said,

"That's A Fact!"

Roach On The Ceiling

It's more fun for me
To write these words
On the closed commode
Staring above
At your clinging body.

Are you upside down?

Are you sick and alone?

The Truths, have you found?

Are you brighter than me?
And,
If so, do I care?

You probably won't answer.
I guess I'll still stare.
Your kind have survived the ages gone.
History is my major.
My future is done.

Never again, will I question you.
Unless you're still here,
When I look up for you.

Photograph by Joe Omelchuck

Photograph by Joe Omelchuck

III. PETS

Who

Who listens most,

The Dog or the Kid?

I'm not a great parent.

I'm not a great master.

They react to my weakness.

They give me Laughter.

I Love them
Both.

All of the time.

I love myself,

When I only ask why.

I Love Fleas

The only nuisance

which keeps me hounded

are my dog's fleas.

I guess I'm grounded;

Ground Hog Day

is my disease.

Alarms are sounding.

It's time to leave

my Happy Home.

Another Time.

We all need Home

And

Love for Life.

Gizmo Spats 1 & 2

1.

I quit my job and started playing;

I started to write and stopped praying.

I got a Dog and lost a carpet.

Yesterday, I bought Bill a socket.

2.

The black hole of humanity is forming.

the choices expanding,

the answers contracting.

Our minds are in rage.

What do we do?

We move so fast we can't relax.

I stand in awe

of Gizmo's Paws.

Dogs Don't Work

*Envy,
they say
is wrong*

*But
I wish I was a Dog*

*with a compassionate Master
who understood*

how

Ruff

it was

to be a Dog

The Tingler / Renaissance

Cold Showers

Long Hours

Short Nights

Gizmo's Right

- - - - -

I've Seen the Beatles

I've Seen the Stones

Men on the Moon

And Home Alone

Nine Lives

Cats supposedly

have nine lives.

So in human years

we share equal times.

7 x 9 = 63.

White or Black,

Grey.

The eyes, green.

A stare with no words.

Only a hiss.

A Purr

If You're Lucky,

Blessed

Is

BLISS.

IV. INDIANS

Photograph by Joe Omelchuck

Border Line

Red River

Pool

of

Blood.

Cherokee

Puddle,

Tomahawk

Song.

Manifest Destiny,

Womanfest, too.

These Rights are a Given

But Taken from You.

So Confucius.

So lost.

The end of this page

Will never die.

Who What Where When Why If

I know

That
I
Am Special.

I know

That
You
Are Too.

In this Dream

Called

Life,

We Are

All

The

Chosen

Few.

The Eagle Has Landed

Fire.

The Eagle

Has

Landed.

NO Wind

NO Earth.

NO Air.

NO Water

Footprint on the MOON.

MAN!

Did You See It?

DREAM

COME

TRUE.

White Eagle.

V.OTE

V. POLITICS

Year Of The Busch
or
Is Addiction a Reflection
Of Our Crazy Earth

I'm glad it's over.
The Year of the Busch.
The snow's on the mountain.
Not in my town.

But He's coming back here.
Have you heard?
Read my lips.
Stay clear of the ex-presidents.
Many are here.

They make more money than most of us
For doing nothing.
They're still covered, by secrets I mean.
The Service is Provided
By Our Tax Dollars,
I think.

He's not a crook, he told me so.
With his hands raised, he stole the show.
Money for his tapes, I can't believe.

The World Is Crazy.

Consistent

At Least.

Pentagon vs. Pentangle

They take your Tax Dollars.
Make War and Pain.
Charge $50.00
For a nickel nut made.
Build a Church
To hide in.

They'll run, but can't hide
From the hell that they're in.
They won't
Be Alive
'Til they become
Their own Best Friends.

Should I pay my Tax Dollars
With these items listed:
A Hammer, A Nail,
A Screw or a Twistee?

I don't think so.
They would crucify me,
Or nail me up
For caring to care.

Their faces need Names
So the Truth will come.
There is plenty
for All

If We ALL Love ALL.

The Hole

I'm glad you can't
smell me,
the day I
built this.
The weather was muggy
but the rain cooled
like bliss.

In the heat of the moment,
this hole was created
and
now Death will come,
as you rip it to shreds.
So smell this instead.

The words of a fool.
He didn't inhale.

But he lied.
Just like you.

Guess his name,
in the year which you live.

(KW)
(Kill A What?)

When you're perceived as a critic,

They will argue with you.

No doubt about it.

Words are confused.

They weren't there.

They didn't see

The way that it happened.

How can they perceive?

Two sides of the story.

A Civil War.

Speak your own mind.

Will there always be War?

NAFTA

or

Night Asks For The Answer

It

is

light.

The opposite side.

Debate

this.

Why?

Why not?

So.

So what.

I'm on a Mexican, oh oh

Radio.

No Trabaho. ho ho.

B.S. In Politics

I flunked Political Science

At U of H Main Campus.

Now I'm glad I did.

A B.S. for me won't happen.

Politics is bullshit.

Presidents are Puppets.

They collate information,

Then blurt out words of nothing.

Now I'm Pissed

Fire
is the motive for condemning
two cool souls
because they push your buttons.
So now you call cool cruel.

I guess you want a motive
for being
unaware
of what
is going on.

I'd see you in the past life,
by then
I will
be gone.

So if you want to see me,
summer is your home.

They say I can't vote
because I haven't registered.

But if I could vote
it would end like this:
Beavis & Butthead in 69.

96 will do
'cause the future has
no mind.

End of Politics/Sportscast

Hindus	3
Muslims	2+1
Nazis	0
Jews	Dead
Bosnians	2
Serbs	2
Protestants	4
Catholics	4
Indians	1
Americans	1 billion
Ruskies	7
Afghanistans	8
Republicans	0
Democrats	0

Photograph by Joe Omelchuck

VI. SPORTS

Forward Pass

My Dad was Irish
and also a Catholic.
Cheer, Cheer for ol' Notre Dame.
We kneeled with our rosaries.
I was at Putt-Putt when It happened.

He died while working, doing the lawn.
Probably sweating, his blood pressure wrong.
Knute Rockne was his hero, I know.

The first forward pass, I pray I will know.
Above the rim is where I should be.
If you think you can catch me,
then think just like me.

Houston will win, if I live my dream.
I pray this will happen.

I guess we'll see.

The Blitz

You never knew what hit you.

I doubt you'll ever forget.

In words like David or Howard Stern,

It's in your face.

Ascend.

Tackle all your guards.

Change their positions.

Call the team psychiatrist.

It's included in your ticket.

Birth And Death In Houston

With No Major Sports Win

When you've been on the edge
and made it back,
keep a piece with you.
It's been your path.

Pleasure and pain
will never be gone
from this world we're in.
We must be strong.

We must share faith
and sing a song.

Angels will guide us
on and on.

In Case I Die

Cremate what's left.
Ashes in an urn.

Please give it to the first team
when Houston is first.

It must be in

Baseball,

Football

or

Hoop.

Things come in threes.
Have you heard?

The birds know the score.
A shortstop I am.
Deep in the hole.
Absorbed with the plan.

To respond in an instant.
Move in a rhythm.
Sacrifice my body.
I'm there every minute.

Something about it.
We all need a game
to remind us about life
and lead us home.

Ticker Tape Day
(12/11/93) (6/24/94)

Do I pray I'm still alive,
when D-Day comes?
The day a Houston sports team
has the balls it takes to come.

Kill without guilt.
If only for one time.
A national Texas holiday
inscribed
for all the time
that anyone remembers.

Pyramid of games.
They say things come in threes.
Birth & Death in Houston.

I've met Rudy;
through him, this day we'll see.

Will there be a book of history
of the human race?
Will there be a gridiron, diamond,
3 point line and saves?

If I knew, I'd tell
and not lead you on.
So instead, I'll break
and shut up.
Faith is weak.
The son is strong.

6/22/94 – Dedicated to the Houston Rockets
1994 NBA Champions

Photograph by Joe Omelchuck

VII. RELIGION

Philism

I flew;

up off the ground.

So others

came around.

I said,

"Don't start a religion,

around me."

They said,

"We'll see."

Religion

Death Happens.
This body leaves.
Life goes on.

Some will grieve.
Others don't,
Until it's time
For them to experience
That point in time,
When a friend goes:
A wife, a son,
A mother, a husband,
A lover, a pup.

Religion gives hope
That after we're gone
Our souls keep on going.

But religions share harm.
They fight for their rituals.
Fight for beliefs.
Fight without knowing
That we all share belief,

In something beyond us.
That which we can't know,
Until we share it.

This body won't know.
I'll leave you with this:
A thought and a prayer.

Get it together.
Religion's not there.

Redwood Sanctuary

I Don't Want a New Religion.
God. Man. Together. Sold.
The Sign Says.
Merge in Soul.
Black, White.
Truth.
Red, Right?
Hope So.
PRAY
Grey Ate Redwood Forest.

Sanctuary

A large percentage of spirits on earth.
Consumed by religion.
A soul and body hurt.
Was it the dark ages,
When the concept was formed,
That a church is ground for
Sanctuary?

Is that why many sprint to their doors?
Never is forgot
That family of trees.
The Redwood Clan is My
Sanctuary.

White Eagle.

Vatican Explosion

FIRE

FIRE

Burned to the ground.

If you believe in spirit.

The Redwood Forest

Is my Cathedral.

Avoid the Drive-In Tree.

Tourist Trap.

Get to the silence

Amidst the Family.

Seeds planted

Home on the Earth.

For Those Who Don't Know

                Join
                the
                Crowd
                in
                this
                together.
                Not
                special,
                but
                loud
                and
                pissed
                at
                our
                Maker.
His⇨   Puzzle   ⇦Her
                sucks.
                Boys
                and
                girls
                need
                home.

                White Eagle

Photograph by John Lee

VIII. DEVILS

Devils

I stood up to the Devils
in my life.
I acknowledged their wisdom.
I lived their fright.
They will be with me in a different form.

Peace of mind comes
when you least expect it.
Ride it now, and when it's gone
the devils will come,
but they'll give you a song.

I've lived with the devils
in this world that I'm in.

I've lived their experience,
I won't call it sin.

Take It or Leave It.
Do you have a choice?

Ride the wave;
Live through your storm.

Photograph by Joe Omelchuck

IX. ANGELS

Flying

Angels I sense,
but do not see.

Flying's my dream
if I just see
that worry won't help
or change a thing
in the past
that's not here,
but it could be.

I ask for help
and ignore the pain
with D N A.

I can't even write it.
Why do I feel shame?
In the morning light,
it doesn't seem right,
but I do it again.

White light is the sequence
that clears thoughts of sin.

The moment is here,
I want to be near;
the end I don't fear,
make it clear.

I Pray.
Past.
Present.
Future.
FLY ME TODAY.

Photograph by Joe Omelchuck

X. MY CHILD

The Earth Is Flat

They called it flat,
I've experienced that.
You can jump off
and fall and fall.
You will be caught,
'cus spirit's round,
in spite of all that
pounds and pounds.
When the sun is up
and the sun is down,
when responsibility calls,
you heed the sound.
You don't know why,
you only thank
and day to day,
you live to pay and pray
and give, not take,
for that's more fun.
I bless the day
that she was born.

Papa

Alone Not Together

Dave Mason I'm not.
Lost in myself.
Pain of my thought.

No rhyme or reason.
No explanation.
No relief seen.
No room to breathe.

Future is lurking
All is a dream.

The earth moves
faster than thought.

Last night was my birthday.
The eclipse I saw.
Full Moon Fever.

Cab home.
Forty-five dollars.
Gas line was broke.

But My Daughter slept well.

11/29/93

A – Mongolians

The Mongolians are a'coming.
B & B will pay them to fly.

Circus on MTV.
Ballerinas are a'flying.

Every year
for years are years.

We go up to the circus
where people live their fears.

I have with me my net;
a web that is so strong.

It's the essence of the answer
which my body shall never know.

Turmoil is my nature.
Somehow I must be strong.

Reason To Live

Not

Knowing

Helps

Me

Breathe.

Shabd

Is

My

Life.

Her

I

Conceived.

Everyday

Everyday
I think of her.

This world is strange.
Of that I'm sure.

She and I may sometimes hurt.
But most of life will be real good.

Give us strength, faith and hope.
Give us friends and words of love.

And when we're sad, down and out,
Make us think, twist and shout.

Hurt no one, though we feel pain.
Together we will conquer.

To Shabd

It's hard to begin
when the end has no end.
Words can't express
your sweet caress.

I've experienced love
for all time.
There's no one else whose heart
is part mine.

It's not hard to write these lines.
We both know it's for all time.

Whatever we do,
wherever we go,
I'll always be there
and you'll always know.

Papa

10th Birthday Prayer

I pray write now
to always share with you
this special day.

By the grace of the angels,
I've always been there.

April 20th.
The day you appeared
from your womb of comfort.
Your eyes made me live.

As the years pass,
they seem like days.

Our current of love
gives the ocean waves.

We'll ride it out
Day to Day.

When our breath is gone,
our souls will stay.

Papa

Over The Cliff

Baptist Church excursions
on the bus.

Lots of children,
worlds of love.

A time in space,
your child is gone.

The bus goes over.
Your world is wrong.

I don't know why,
I won't blame God
or say His will
is why this comes.

Take me where
there is no clock.

My daughter's love
is this soul's heart.

Papa

Drop

I am a name dropper,
But I can't remember names.

A different way to express the story.
Is it really just the same?

Pop a top again.
Thoughts unfold the glory.

This pen is automatic.
Standard is this story.

She stubbed her toe today
outside a trailer in Magnolia.

Pleasures
never outbalanced
by the pain
they both have showed me.

Papa

Mid Night X Mass

Christmas

Love Shabd here.

Christmas Eve.

A Day.

A Year.

Sit on His Knee.

Make a Wish.

Material Wants.

Fly in the Sky.

You won't be Alone.

Rain Dear.

Question.

Alone.

Relative-ity

The essence of Now
is in your mind.
It's only for you.
You're one of a kind.

Each moment you feel,
each moment you breathe,
is what you perceive.
It's that which you see.

Shabd is special.
One of a kind.

The kind I'm in love with.
Hear these words rhyme.

One day I'll be gone,
and she will too.

Love has no end.
Do you know it's true?

Papa

TO SHABD

IT'S Hard To Begin
when the end has no end.
Words can't express, your
sweet caress.

I've experienced Love.
For ~~the very~~ all ~~Fust~~ Last Time

There's no one else ~~whose heart~~
~~like you, us friend~~ is part ~~more~~
~~makes me feel this fine~~ mine.
~~can write there poem~~

It's not hard To write
these lines.
We Both Know its for all Time
Whatever we do, wherever we go.
I'll always be there.
& you'll always Know.

Papa. 6/3/92

My Daddy

My daddy I love
forever and foever
HQS always there
for me and that.
my definition of
my daddy

Shala

2. HQS very nice
loving and caring
there from the day
I appeared and
thats my def. of my
daddy
Shala

XI. HER TO ME

My Father

I love my
father very much. He's
sweat and cheerful
but that's not much.
He's all that a little girl
could want he's kind.
He's got a mind. He's
loveable and very
hugable but most
of all he's my father
and I'm his daughter
and that's all a little girl
could want.

By: Shabd
To: Daddy

My Daddy

1. My daddy I love
forever and foever.
He's always there
for me and that's
my definition of my daddy.

2. He's very nice
loving and caring
there from the day
I appeared and
that's my def of my
daddy.

Shabd

Photograph by Joe Omelchuck

Photograph by Joe Omelchuck

XII. CHILDREN

A B C's

Notes & Chords,
Words and Music
Swords & War.
Bombs & Home.
Love & Hate.
Them & Us.
Me & You.
Alone.

Thru.
Tunnels are dark & they close in.
Bad dreams of wells.
A child so dear.
She was saved from the pit.
Everyone watched and prayed for her.
Her experience was hell.
We held her near.

Ask her some day if she remembers.
Hypnotize her if she can't
We've all had the feeling.

So leave her alone
and talk to yourself.

Leavemealone.

Life is itself.

*Adam Lost,
A Damn Loss.
America's Least Wanted.*

Your child was abducted and murdered in pain.
You lecture and preach to get rid of the pain.
But I don't blame you, what would I do?
This world is so crazy.
So troubled and lost.

I look to the ocean,
the trees
and the frost.

You're one of a kind,
not really.
Many have experiences this crazy.

So you tell us on Friday,
or Sunday one year.
The days are the same.
Now the end you don't fear.

Why should I watch this?
When all I need do,
is open my door
and pray it's not true.

Neighbors

People across the street,
I do not know their names.

What we call poetry
is verbalizing pleasure and pain.
With a piece of a tree and a writing utensil,
words change; thoughts universal.

Getting back to the point,
I heard something special.
I saw it all in the words of the innocent.
My ears heard the cry.

"Papa!"
this little form screamed
as if there were no tomorrow.
Papa was gone in a car that I saw.
The moment was clear.
So sweet and so dear.

Her mom held her close and closed the door.
Maybe they slept,
maybe they dreamed.
The love of a child,
is a dream in a dream.

Photograph by Joe Omelchuck

XIII. SEX

Homework

Class has finished
Forever.
Alice knows.
Siamese twins.
Look in my glass,
See the hole.
Acid made it.

Will I enter a tunnel,
Or land in a well.
Claustrophobic rubble.

I think I'm a puppet.
Call a spade a spade.

If I'm made in Your image,
I guess You've been laid.

(This experience is about helping my daughter do her homework and also about Alice Cooper and Alice in Wonderland, who were Siamese twins, LSD, Life after life, Children stuck in wells, Puppets, Cards, God & Sex.)

Photograph by Joe Omelchuck

XIV. CARDS

Gin

Win or Lose.

It's just a Game.

One on One.

I Pray You're Safe.

Your Voice I Savor.

You Give Me Joy.

The Afterlife,

Can Not Be Told.

Photograph by Joe Omelchuck

XV. FRIENDS

Annette O'Toole

Race to the blackboard
And grab the white chalk.

Show them you're special.
I've sang many songs.
And you have too.

In far out lands,
L.A.'s on the fault line
Of grammar and math.

Who will win
This game of life,
You or I?

Ponder thoughts of
Truth, Lies.

If there's an answer
To what we seek,

Why is it hidden?

'Cause Life is sleep.

Cruz

Your eyes reveal
the secret

that I ponder
in my quest.

Last night was
so very special.

Do you think
it was the best?

When our bodies
have turned to dust

and there's no
such thing as lust,

My soul
will not forget

The beauty
that we felt.

Recycle Man/
St. Nick – A Christmas Gift

One day I awoke,
and struggled to work.
I was leaving the house
and noticed a quirk.

A Black man had opened
the trash bag I left.
Cans from previous days
were most of the fest.

My head was pounding,
but I had to go.
I started to feel guilty,
but then came the show.

We started to talk,
and I gave him a smile.
He makes no mess,
and knot's always tied.

He's old and strong,
tall and thin.
He moves real slow,
but he'll give you a grin.

He drives his old truck
and makes his rounds.
I'll miss him tomorrow
if he's not around.

In the conversation,
he made me think.
There were so many cans.
He said "You've made my day."

J. B. McCoy

You have a name of steel
And I remember a body to match.
I'm sure you worked real hard.
Every day you earned your cash.

I don't know all the details,
Of how you lived your life.
I pray that death will relieve you
From life's worry and it's strife.

As you gaze upon us
From your home with those above,
Guide us through this turmoil
And give us all your love.

I pray that you can hear me.
My faith is very strong.
Do You Love or Like Her?
This question is my song.

In Memorial to the Real McCoy J.B.

12 10 93

Remember
the
Day?

We left a home.

Moved in a
U-Haul Truck.

Why
Do I feel so alone?

When friends appeared,
In a special order,
To assist in our journey,
Tears prompt this story.

It must be ironic
when I look down and see
a Catch 22.

The carpet's the same.

Lost Comb = Lost Awareness

Less
than
a
buck.

Insignificant
amount.

I
feel
so
ashamed.

I
miss
you

and
How.

The Boat

Beyond this world,
they call to me.

But in this world,
responsibility.

A tug of war,
I'm in the middle.

Extremes for me,
so I must riddle.

Learning to listen
and learning to ride.

Not inspired to vote,
won't give up and hide.

Friends keep appearing again
and again.

Your prayers will be answered,
if giving's your friend.

For Hari & Me (Huddy)

When it gets too weird
and it's the time to change.

Don't pack your bags,
just stake your claim.

On your heart and soul,
you'll do what's right.

Your inner voice
will be the light.

Hands Shake

Hands Shake

Like an old soul.

I'm coming back,
I have been told.

I'm glad they know

and share this fact.

Love and friends

we all should have.

Bless Me Father

Bless Me Father

For I have grinned.

It's been,

"Light Years"

since my last

confession.

These

are

my

friends.

Jeff & Laticia

The key to a relationship
was formed years ago.

The goals are the same,
the path, quite, quite insane.

She shoots and she writes.
Her words never bite.

He's not quite the same,
but we know it's a game.

I'm glad I was there
to share, it's no struggle.

I appreciate their relationship
for mine are in trouble.

Who Was That Masked Man

WHO WAS THAT MASKED MAN?

NO.

ZORRO

Frogs

Jump

around

me,

You

short term

beings.

I've

lived

much

longer

than

you.

Teach

me

All.

Although

you're

small.

Lips

You never unlearn

the things you master.

I thought this day

would be a disaster.

But Lips came through

and shared content.

The Weasels were there

and didn't repent.

Yet.

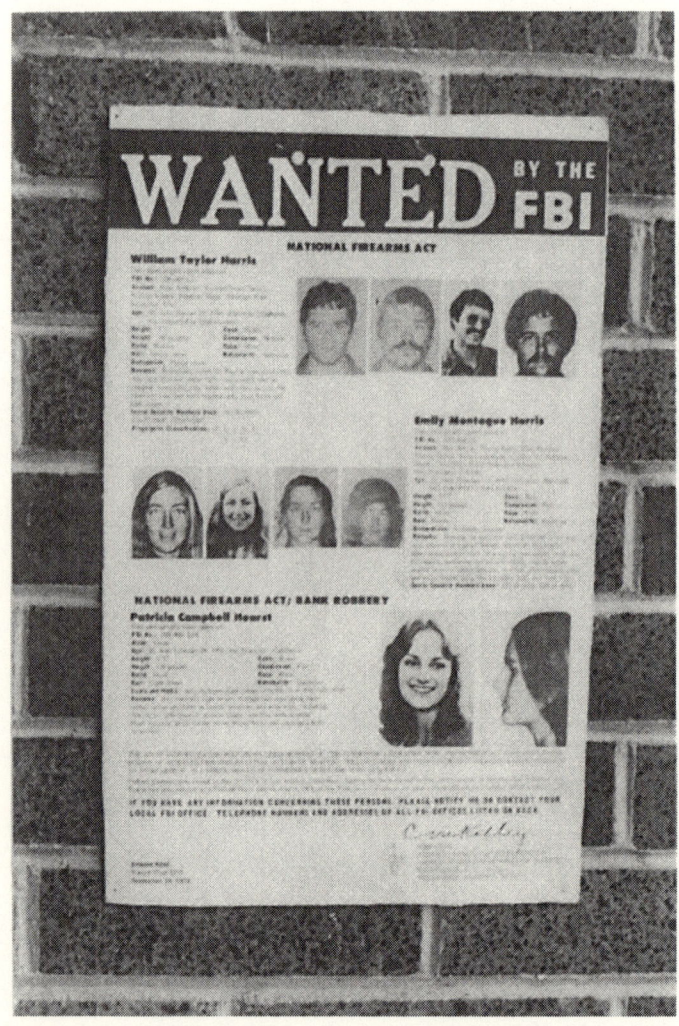

Photograph by Joe Omelchuck

XVI.
STEALING A WANTED POSTER
OF PATTY HEARST
FROM THE
DOWNTOWN POST OFFICE –
A MISDEMEANOR

The Wind

A crazed hippie downtown,
he seized the moment
with many around.

They were not looking
or did not care.

He plucked her from
a wall right there.

Now you see her,
so please do stare.

Want a piece?
I'll take you there.

Seize the moment.
Fuck fear.

Ride the waves;

The wind is clear.

Photograph by Joe Omelchuck

XVII. CONFUSION / SAY

No #

This day is numbered.
Each day is the same.

There are always two beings
who experience the same pain.

There are two more,
in pleasure exact.

There is no earth being
I've met
to explain that fact.

You know why I question?

What is there I need?

I spit on your puzzle.

Share with me.

Please.

Puppets

That's the word.

First and last.

No strings attached.

Love to
Laugh
Cry.

RIGHT.

The shorter, the better.

We're puppets of Life.

Skeletons

Friday the 13th.

August 13, 1993.

We share skeletons
in our closets.

Stones don't throw.

If not, you'll see
that we share

the pain of life,
pleasures,

Hand in Hand.

It's the imbalance
that I wish
that I could understand.

Input

Each Experience,
of all the souls on earth,
now affects my brain.

You think this sounds absurd?

If not, just read the paper,
subscribe and you will pay.

Or turn on channel 2
at 6pm each day.

Now you understand.

If grey is your school's color,
does it really matter?

This life has made me Wonder.

L A T E

↗ Long Ago Three Eyes ↖

converged
to
form
a

↑ ▲ ↑

Vibrating
in
Your mind

The
eye
within
the storm.

Not to be explained,
not to be discussed,
not to be debated;
Only to be us.

Alone I will not be.
I have no cross to share.
My essence I deem pure.
If so, I'll take you there.

↑ ↑

See you in the next world
and don't be

↖ ↗

Convenience Stores

Life is fast
and often short,
for those who work there.

Have they a choice?
I don't know.

But I know them,
they're often kind
and often friends.

They speak weird English.
I'm not bilingual
so I salute them.

They've lived through evil.
So they don't fear society's curse.

Each day is special.
Eternity yours.

La Strada
(August 16, 1992)

Sun's Out
And It's Raining.

I Cry
When I Laugh.

Can You Explain It?

Morning

Think about the loss,

Before it happens.

Don't forget to floss,

I've seen it happen.

Appreciate it now

For what it's worth.

Time will tell

Our point of birth.

Check Out

Mirrors are used
for a reason.

When it comes time
then look.

A moment in time,
for only you.

If your word is not constant
your life has more curves.

These words have meaning,
the middle I need.

For extremes only pull us,
when it's time to be freed.

Tears

If you don't sweat,
You cry.

If you don't cry,
You fry.

You pace the floors.
You lock the doors.

Tomorrow it will be different.

Butt the same.

PA

North Fork.
If you saw Rifleman
on TV,

the cry of a child
gave you a seed

of appreciation
for life on the edge.

A blink is the time
of a bullet's life span.

Death brought eyes alive,

Currents of love. From the other side.

Xcess

The road to Excess leads

…

To the bathroom.

Laws

Should I feel guilty
when white snow propels me?

Keep track of the bills,
all the responsibilities.

But don't get caught up
in bullshit things.

Laws have come,
but they're relative
to that which is happening
in your own world.

How can I say
what I feel?

You have to start
with creation's truth;

Think you.

Bottoms Up

From the depths of our souls,
There's no where to go butt up.
So here's to us.

Gutter calls. Zero pins.
Ashamed. No score.
No where to go butt up.

The lucky ones survive the pit,
Sing to tell and share hell.
There, Satan rules, where there are none.

No school.
Graduation Day.
You are alone.

Friends can't help you.
There is no home.

Too many words for one lifetime.
That's the reason for song.

It has limit
With no boundary.

Finite vs. Infinite

Finite vs. Infinite equals (=)
Love

♥

Between Two (2)
Words

< >

Lies the Human Race.

A beginning
with no end.

Lost.
But saved.

+ -

Never understood.
Alive forever.

∞

Fear,
I won't fear.

❽

Death is forever

A
Live.

○
12794
Full Moon Phil

L.A.

Earth Quakes
Everything happens first
in L.A.

Tremors move east.
Don't go west, young one.

Be aware of the signal.

Everything happens first
in L.A.

Wrath of life.

Mud and Fire.

Bigotry and Hate.

Need and Sun.

Cold Water.

Katharine's need.

Clockwork of
Storm

Warm.

I've seen Spencer and Dick.

Remember When

Remember When …

Choices were few,

Chevy or Ford.

New or used.

TV channels

One, Two, Three.

AB,
NB,
CBS.

Photograph by Joe Omelchuck

Sounds of Music

When the band bites,

When the crowd stinks,

When they charge you a cover,

When you're too stoned to think,

These are a few of my nightmares

Each Week.

Photograph by Joe Omelchuck

Drawing by Bryan Kilburn

XVIII. ME, MYSELF & I

Whatever, And That's Me

I don't need Satan. I don't need Jesus.
Loving myself season to season
is
what I need.

Then I can share, give and care.
Satan's too evil, God's too good.
So put me in the middle
Understood.

Whoever is listening,
Maybe it's me.
Come on now,
It's time to be freed.

If life's a dream and we're all asleep,
Turn on the alarm so I can leave.
Put it on the radio, don't need no buzz.

Give me a song, transition is fun.

I must be snoozing, but that's fun.
I won't get up, until the fun comes
and that's me!
And
I'm a glutton for
Funishment.

Look it up
In your Funk & Wagnels.

Socks

Sorting socks;
line 'em all up.

Be prepared
for annoyment.

You'll lose one.
Too much for me.

Where is my maid?

Can't afford her.
'Cause I live in the shade.

The Answer

One answer
to
One question.

Let's ponder together
the eternal message.

On the tip of my tongue.
On the twilight of sleep.

I'll nod to all beings,
unless they are creeps.

I'll figure it out
Reel Quick.

A moment's a moment.
Don't slip.

Teach your children.

Teach your self.

Share it together.

Give yourself.

Never Alone
or
We're All In This Together

Don't look around.

Don't look behind.

Don't look ahead.

Close your eyes.

All together,

Pleasure and pain.

Different bodies,

One and the same.

How can it not be?

It may seem strange.

The other options

Give me more pain.

Ground Zero / Starting At The Top

The bills are paid.
The house is gone.

VISA, Am Ex, Bank A
Still strong.

Starting over
at the top.

Credit, no limit,
Must not be wrong.

I've never been the type
to plan far ahead.

In fact, each day I wonder
and question,
"What is next?"

Karma

If Karma is instant,
Does it need boiling water?
It must have caffeine,
Or I won't even bother.

Light is a rip off.
Buy whole milk instead.

Then cut it with whatever,
You decide.

Fat's not the problem
In my Life.

Light brings noises,
Confusion galore.
Dark scales down,
Less is more.

If you buy my book,
You receive a plenary indulgence,
Join my crusade.

It's a deduction.
Well, maybe not.
Rules change.

The IRS should be served on a plate.

Join the Baptists.

OM
(Where The Heart Is)

In the Beginning

was the word.

You've heard it at night.

The station turns off.

A buzz gives you fright.

You're still awake

when most sleep.

You are not alone.

You fucking creep.

A Prayer For Phil

TO WHOM IT MAY CONCERN:

I want to give, I've felt that feeling,
When you don't worry about self,
Your mind has less reeling.

Is Mother Teresa a case in point?
I'd like to ask her.
Help me, just point.

Give me the strength to alter my habits.
I just need to start;
It's as simple as that.

All I desire is to live in my heart.
A day to day thing.
I will start.

I've done it before and it happened so slow.
A subtle thing,
But now there is snow.

The turkey is cold but my life will be warm.
I'll radiate heat
And help with their storm.

Experience was pleasure and frightening pain.
I thank the Giver.
This body was made.

The ball's in my court, so I'll take my best shot.
My Ego be gone.
Flight will start.

Competition

Welcome all you judges
Now you've read my stuff.
Would you like to hear it?
And see it one on one?

Pictures will have to do.
For the sweaty masses.
Politics and religion, I've failed.
I've felt their passion.

Sucked in many times.
Until no energy left.
Then you listen.

People often pray
When they reach this condition.

Should I sink this low
Or should I rise so high.

Presumptions are a trap
I will have the hidden side.

Condominium

Where
is
the
Time
and
Space
Continuum

That
I
Know
and
Love?

Everywhere.

Angel's Puppet

I am
the Angel's Puppet.

Om
Bilical
Chord.

Bunjee
Dude.

Sold
the Farm

In Kansas.

Aunt Eileen
Died
Yesterday.

Photograph by Joe Omelchuck

Byzantine Empire

The World and those there
are close to predecessors.

Time.
Souls and Bodies Share.

Limelight is Timed.

Cinceunta Minuetos.

So Fast, So Weird.

Thought.

Will I be the Next

In
The Limelight?

Photograph by Joe Omelchuck

Red, White and Black

TANTRA.

Sex, Drugs, Rock & Roll.

Pure and Evil.

Need:
Soul.

Have a Heart.

Need a Life

Without
Pain.

Yeah.

Write.

Color
Blind.

3/4/94

Mo Ho Tells

OK
I'm a Sag. ↗

I like to travel

On my high horse

In the sky.

I like to see people

And look in their

Eyes.

Winter Simmers

Giving is receiving.
Never content.

Never at ease,
Life is extreme.

Sometimes,
There is a breeze.

Breath.

Breathe.

Fresh air.

Give it away.

CO_2
You

In the next breath.

We'll all be late.

Dust

I've experienced love.
I've experienced lust.

I've experienced trust
and swept up dust.

This body is here
as I speak to you.

It will be gone
and I'll be new.

Not the same,
another name.

Perhaps a tree,
a rock, a leaf,

Or something else
you have not seen.

Tonight,
I'll feel it

In the dream.

Secret

Revealed.

I will share

A secret
With you.

There are
No secrets.

No proud
And few.

No war.
No pain.

Only love
For all and you.

Three Meals A Day

Breakfast
Lunch
and
Dinner.,

Then
There's
Snoring.

One's
A
Meal
Will
Do.

The Last Supper.

P.S. Be Here Then
For Baba Ram Dass

My poetry reflects
the fact that I live
on the earth
in that reality.

And I know there's more;
another reality.

A blending of both
is what I seek.
The truth is there.
Sometimes I'm weak.

Everyone has a style.

You don't need
to take a course.

You are the course.

Be here then.

Master of Deceit
or
The Art of Lying

A lie is only
For the giver.

Self Inflicted
Pain Delivered.

You are your words.
Sow your say.

You must deliver
your word

Or PAY.

Poetry - - The Motion

A poem

is a

piece

of the

puzzle.

Actions speak louder than words.
Silence is never absurd.

You'll know what I feel.
When you never conceal

that love

is the

only thing

real.

Nats On Life

These little jingles
left and right brain.

If I separate
my left and right
brain for too long,

I get too involved
in one or the other.

So my lines
quasi reflect a balance
of left and right.

Philosophical,
Esoteric,
and everyday Life.

OR

In I'm Balance.

Time To Bite

Occasionally,
I get an itch.

To bite of my nails,
A protein twitch.

Spit it out.

Grow anew.

Process of growth
and re-generation.

On the stove.

Toe Nail Stew.

Photograph by Joe Omelchuck

Rat Race

Tired of the rat race;
I've run out of gas.
Suburbia can't balance
Rush hour's path.

I guess I'm a bum,
A beggar, a fool.
I won't sell you a paper.
That's much too cruel.

Your kids might see it,
And copy an action.
A chill it could send you.
I won't start that reaction.

I have a job,
A home and a life.
We have that in common,
But we're one of a kind.

Will you trade me your gold card
For the one I own?
My limit I've paid off.
The card I still own.

Intact.

So Far
Away.

Famousisity

The path to a star
is a ride called
The Dream.

When you know it's time,
you must do your
Own Thing.

Tomorrow

They say
you need a goal
to fulfill
what they term soul.

I can't confirm
that thought.
Another theory
down the trough.

Heading for the tunnel,
they say there is a light.
Many say they're seen it.
Should I believe this time?

Long for peace of mind.
as the children form their minds
based on how they live
and what experiences give.

Greetings

Greetings
From the Left and the Right.

Greetings
From the Day and the Night.

Greetings
From your World and Mine.

Greetings
'Till the end of Time.

Clan Of Kennedy

I hate to watch people
putting on a show
when you know
their heart's not in it.

False smiles.
Blow.

Watching is believing.
Seeing is worse.
Now you feel the pain,
Life's curse.

The Pain Of The Moment

The pain of the moment
Makes me aware.
Each body's alone
And so I must stare
While driving along,
Or sitting inside
Of a bar
Or a bistro,
Or a circus ride.

But each soul is a part,
Of the total experience.
This I pray dearly
To keep me from fearing
The moments of pain,
The moments of grief,
The moments that all souls
Will soon share relief.

News

You can be certain,
That each day,
The news will come
And they will say

A different story
With the same theme.
Is there an end
To pain and greed?

These thoughts are mine,
That's not the question.
Why does this happen?
It's a prerequisite
To total knowledge
Without a duel.

Time astounds me.
Moments scare.
Peace of mind
I pray we'll share.

POET

Prophet

Of

Ethereal

Trite

POEM

Patterns

Of

Ethereal

Mist

The Thinker

Do Bee
Do Bee Do Bee
Do Bee.

Life of Riley.
TV.
Creation of Man.

Or does God create things?

Puzzle this
in spare time.

If you're part
of the puzzle,

Are there lines
in your hand?

Share.

For Denise/Grasshopper

I left the bar early.
Went home and hugged my dog.
The alarm was preset
My lover had called;

Several times.

Her words were special
And they didn't rhyme.
But they rang
I miss you, she said.

Denise,
Before I took time
To write these words,
I experienced a shudder
Of a flying bird.

Thought in my mind,
Of a tree roach.
Then I caught a glimpse
Of green.

I cringed in my bed.
Dog didn't move.
Then I made a vow
I will save you.

Turned on the light
And picked up a shoe.
Trapped him or her in it
With a note.
Opened the door
With the shoe from the ground.

Mama Got The Belt

I have this real nightmare.
When I was a kid,
Four years young.
I was at church with Mom.

She was eating bread on her knees
And there was a fence
Between her and this guy.
She opened her mouth
And he gave her a little circle.

I ripped the prayer book
To shreds.
She came back to our pew.
It was on the right side
Of the center aisle
About five rows from the front.

She grabbed my arm
And took me home
And got out the belt.

A Brief History of Rhyme

Secrets of snow.
Cold dreams
Mystery.

Dead child
Reunion gone bad.
Thoughts of all
Universe
Glad,
Sad.

Every bad seed
Experience
Felt by all.
Set us free.
Hear our call.

Child Abuse

I was convicted
of child abuse.
I fed my daughter
wrong.
No green things.

LOVE

Homeless In Hyannisport

We Ji Bords.

For

Sale.

I Don't Fight With Food

I can't digest.

So I rarely eat

One meal a day.

So

I don't fight with Food.

Food fights with me.

p.s.
FOOD FIGHT!

Lordy, Lordy, Look Who's Forty
New Life's Resolution

Forty Days and Forty Nights.
No alcohol,
No drugs,
No white light.

You call it fright,
We'll see who's right.

I will fly.
It's my dream.
I share faith,
It's not a scheme.

Men and women –
Pause.

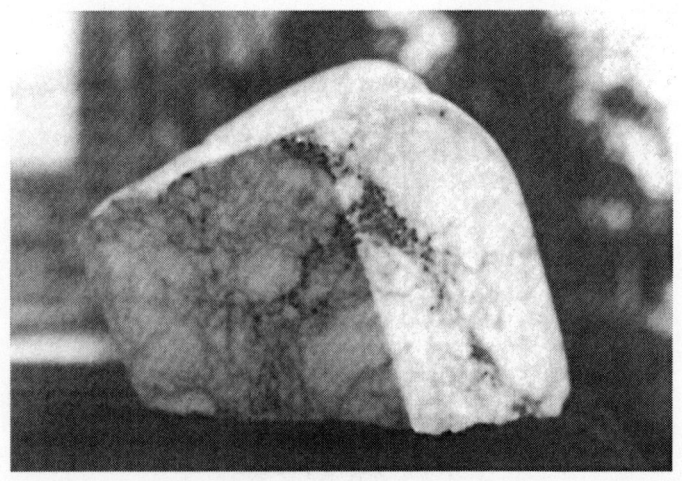

Photograph by Joe Omelchuck

XIX. GOD AND JESUS

Tools Of The Trade

Do you think
That it's ironic
To be done in
With the tools of your trade?

Hammer time with nails.
No blood on your hands.
Only eyes feel the pain,
When you gaze on those below.

As the thunder sounds,
You know the past and future.
As the present sees
Your shroud.

Does every one on earth today
Wonder why it's such a mess?
Can earth ever be in harmony?
No.

Until it's alive while dead
Like you.

Life

Is life a gift
Of an unknown?
Can you explain
What no one knows?

I'll share,
If you'll give.

I'm tired of the clues.

No words 'splains
Your God Damn
Hypocritical
Master Plan.

Empower All With All

Please.

The magic word.

Set us free.

Hesitate

One more time,

I won't be

Your best friend.

Birth And Death Of Jesus

Celebrate life and death
Of a one of a kind.
Truth said.

Born from a virgin.
Not of this world.
An alien space cadet.

Spirit of the bird.
Word given to you and me.

Love
Your neighbor as yourself.

And
God
You will meet.

Rut

Even the good times
are bad.
Jesus lived and died
so we'll have
a lesson to feel
and share
with that soul.

A Father and Mother,
their egg is your soul.
Jesus had nothing.

Do you live in a barn?
On a farm in Kansas?
Do you want to go home?

No being exists
on planet Earth
who's not given shelter
and loved when hurt.

Jesus Or Hammer Time

Knock on wood.
Sorry bad joke.
You deserve it.
"Holy Ghost."
Lightning strike me.
Odds are better
Than winning Lotto.
I don't need money.
Can't buy me Luv.

The Envelope

Have you ever closed
The envelope.
Thought you'd finished,
Licked the fold.
A time later
Very close.
It doesn't matter.
Sealed shut.
Get the tape and pray.
The same mistake,
I'll surely make.

Baba Ga Noose

Eggplant in a blender.
Throw in a sesame seed.

The street of no return.
One way.

The sign I see,
Love and hate.
Dream.

Ism's

Be gone away.
Like the dust of the ages.
You've had your day.

See their distraction.
Life's a pity.
They worship Jesus.
'Cause he's lived pain
And takes ours
Always
In his name.

I am a one
Who questions your ways.
You shared your knowledge.
Pleasure needs pain.

SADOMASA-ISM.

Home

There is a reason.
There is an answer.
There is a higher power.

Compassion rules,
Tears cool,
The heat of your hour.

A glimpse is felt.
Seen by all
A noticed note.

Home, it's called.

Listerine

Burning light.
Day.
Experience the pain,
Pleasure.
You'll soon say
There is no substitute
When a teacher
Makes your day.

The Meaning Of Christmas

Who is Santa?

Pause.

Listen.

Jingle this thought.

He's the father above.

Flying with gifts.

Some are material.

One is perpetual.

A flame

In his eyes.

Twinkle.

Here And There

I don't eat.
I don't sleep.
But,
I can cook.
And sing a lull-a-bye
In a jail
with no bars.

The longest Day,
A star
We all are.

No one is exempt
From merging with me.

God
Already told you,
You're created by
Me.

We're all in this together.
So lighten up and sing
A Christmas Carol.

One plus one
Is
One.

For What I Don't Know

You make me question,
When I need an answer.

It's bugging me often.
The moment must happen,
Very soon.

Persistence is mine.
We don't have a choice.

I'm one of a kind.
You will give me your voice

To share.

The Eyes Don't Have It

Beauty of life.
Lies again.
Pain unfolds.

Does God grin?
I hope so.
The joke's on us.

If we have a third eye,
God must be first.

So who comes in second?
Devils the world.

Upper Level Disturbance

7th CHAKRA
Quake.

Earth be gone.
Abierto.
Por favor.

All for one,
One for all,
Teacher said.

God and me,
Me and God,
Are one.

Art by Denise Lawrence

Photograph by Joe Omelchuck

XX. MY FIRST AND LAST WILL AND TESTAMENT

My First And Last Will And Testament

To Creator, Light Giver, Ultimate Lover, All Knower, Brother, Sister, Father, Mother, etc. – My gratitude
To Shabd – Material stuff and Gizmo Spats, love and angels, including me.
To Brother Bill – All the mountains, rivers, oceans, ashrams and bars you've taken me to.
To Sister – Faith and perseverance
To Dad – The baseball from the best catch I ever made. Remember.
To Mom – The speaker and cord that I accidentally drove off with drunk from the drive-in movie that I went to the night you bought me the new 1970 Dodge Challenger for graduation and $60 for the repair on the left rear fender when I hit the pole that the speaker was attached to and you paid for the next working day.
To All My Friends – As much love, luck and experience that I've had.
To The IRS – A painful death.
To The Earth – A pleasant rebirth.
To Rock-N-Roll – It healed my soul.
To The Local Drug Store – Hang in there.
To The End Of The Lines – No need to beware.

Two Birds
Look To The Sky
Hi Come!

If you look to the sky

With regularity,

You will see

Two birds flying

Together.

Intro To Blind Big Cake Carver/ The End Is the Beginning

I heard the birds,
Before I heard the noise.
I saw the trees,
Before I saw the street.

I fly in the sky,
Without opening an eye.
I went to work,
Before I woke up.

It's easy to see,
If you close your eyes,
And let it
B.

Distant cousins please welcome,
From Houston, Texas,
Blind Big Cake Carver
And the Bipeds.

DA DA DANT.

FOR ALL
10/3/94

The words of this book are my efforts to sort out my experiences so far. They are subject to change and individual interpretation. I was born breach on November 28, 1951, at St. Joseph's Hospital in Houston, Texas, and baptized Phillip Owen Daly. Dr. Bukowski delivered me, so they say.

I am a Sagittarius, the most philosophical of all the signs. Moon in Scorpio, Rising Capricorn. I was born in the year of the Rabbit. I was raised Catholic and I x communicated myself and became a Hippie.

Then I became a vegetarian, meditating, card carrying, turban wearing Dude. They called me Captain Karma 'cause my job was to make sure everyone at the ashram did their chores. Then I quit my post, shaved my beard, lost my religion and returned to Captain Beyond records on CD.

Over the years I've learned how to bang nails. My new home became the snow covered mountains in downtown Montrose, Houston, Texas, a stones throw from historic Lola's Blacklight Cavern.

I have a sweet daughter, 2 ex-wives, one dog, two dead black cats named Shadow, a wonderful family and more cool friends than kernels of popcorn in one of those microwavable popcorn packs with fake butter.

I like to listen to live music, dance on one foot, and say unusual things to anybody who'll listen. I have had three names given to me. I don't want any more names. I've seen Jethro Tull four times. I've got freckles on my back 'cause no one told me about sunscreen.

My thanks to my Mom, Dad, Brother, Sister, Daughter; to Debbie Conley, Ann Harper Jones; to Linda C. Stephens, who sacrificed her left brain and part of her right brain to bring these words to the form you see; to Joe Omelchuck, Denise Lawrence, Bryan Kilburn, John Lee, Tom Caullins, Rene Rogers, Gizmo, Lucy, Sarah, and Natalie, the contributing artists and models for our pictures; to Becky Pfeiffer, Jim Lee, Carlene Wagner, Patrick & Sharon and the ashram people; to Dana Bang & the Leo's Family; to Brad Fountain and Bob Mandel; to Ed Sullivan, Lawrence Welk and Tiny Tim; to George Goebel, George Burns, George Busch, George of the Jungle, Yogi Bhajan, Bobby, and Bill Holtz; to my future ex-wives, Tattoo Rick Man, Baba Mukhtananda, who nailed me with a Shakti-POD; to Beans Barton & the Bi-Peds, Feo Y Loco and all the bands that don't suck; to Pope Guido Pepperoni and his pet flying Cardinals. Thanks to all my other friends and ex-lovers. Thank you if you buy this. So long for now. Have a nice night.

        Phillip Owen Patrick Daly
        Siri Nath Singh Khalsa
        White Eagle

Photograph by Joe Omelchuck

*Virgin Birth
Of Our Child*

It came
From you.

All I did
Was affect the
Way it looks.

Phil becomes a Mom.
Linda becomes a Dad.

The opposite of what
Came before.

Male & Female.
Female & Male.
No Distinction.
Pure.

Phil & Linda
Linda & Phil